Oxford basics

Simple Listening Activities

Oxford **basics**

Simple Listening Activities

Jill Hadfield
Charles Hadfield

OXFORD
UNIVERSITY PRESS

Oxford University Press
Great Clarendon Street, Oxford OX2 6DP

Oxford New York
Athens Auckland Bangkok Bogotá
Buenos Aires Calcutta Cape Town Chennai
Dar es Salaam Delhi Florence Hong Kong
Istanbul Karachi Kuala Lumpur Madrid
Melbourne Mexico City Mumbai Nairobi
Paris São Paulo Singapore Taipei Tokyo
Toronto Warsaw

and associated companies in
Berlin Ibadan

OXFORD and OXFORD ENGLISH
are trade marks of Oxford University Press

ISBN 0 19 442168 6

© Oxford University Press 1999

First published 1999
Third impression 2000

All rights reserved. No part of this publication
may be reproduced, stored in a retrieval system, or
transmitted, in any form or by any means, electronic,
mechanical, photocopying, recording or otherwise,
without the prior written permission of Oxford
University Press, with the sole exception of
photocopying carried out under the conditions
described below.

This book is sold subject to the condition that
it shall not, by way of trade or otherwise, be lent,
resold, hired out, or otherwise circulated without
the publisher's prior consent in any form of binding
or cover other than that in which it is published and
without a similar condition including this condition
being imposed on the subsequent purchaser.

Photocopying
The publisher grants permission for the
photocopying of those pages marked 'photocopiable'
according to the following conditions. Individual
purchasers may make copies for their own use or for
use by classes they teach. School purchasers may
make copies for use by their staff and students, but
this permission does not extend to additional
schools or branches.

Under no circumstances may any part of this book
be photocopied for resale.

Illustrations by Margaret Welbank

Typeset by Mike Brain Graphic Design Limited,
Oxford

Printed in Hong Kong

Contents

Foreword
ALAN MALEY

Introduction

Activities
1. Greetings and introductions
2. The alphabet
3. Numbers
4. Telling the time
5. Personal information
6. Countries
7. Nationalities
8. Locating objects
9. Feelings
10. Families
11. Colours
12. Shapes
13. Parts of the body
14. Describing people
15. Clothes
16. Rooms in a flat
17. Furniture
18. In town
19. Directions
20. In the market
21. Shopping
22. Food and drink
23. Leisure activities
24. Daily routines
25. Jobs
26. Housework
27. Abilities
28. Rules: 'must' and 'mustn't'
29. Describing actions 1
30. Describing actions 2

Foreword

There is a formidable range of materials published worldwide for teachers of English as a Foreign Language. However, many of these materials, especially those published in English-speaking countries, assume that the teachers using them will be working with smallish classes and have abundant resources available to them. Also many, if not most, of these materials make implicit culturally-biased assumptions about the beliefs and values of the teachers and learners.

This situation is ironic in view of the fact that the vast majority of English as a Foreign Language classrooms do not correspond at all to these conditions. Typically, classes are large, resources are limited, and teachers have very few opportunities for training and professional development. Also, the cultural assumptions of teachers and learners in many parts of the world may vary quite significantly from those of materials writers and publishers.

This book is an attempt to address this situation. The authors present 30 lessons at elementary level, each with the same methodological framework. The lessons are explained in clear, accessible language, and none of them require sophisticated resources. Instead, they call on the basic human resources which all teachers and learners bring with them to class. The language points covered are ones found in a typical elementary course, and the topics are those which form part of everybody's daily lives, for example families, homes, and leisure activities.

Most importantly, however, the book offers a framework for teachers who lack training and support. The hope and the expectation is that such teachers will begin by following each step of a lesson quite closely but, as their confidence increases, will adapt and add to the techniques presented here, responding to the particular needs and abilities of their learners.

This is an important book: one of the few attempts to address the problems of the 'silent majority' of teachers worldwide who have little or no training, and few resources to work with.

ALAN MALEY
Assumption University
Bangkok, Thailand

Introduction

English is taught all over the world, by all sorts of teachers to all sorts of learners. Schools and classrooms vary enormously in their wealth and their provision of equipment. Learners are very different from place to place. But, whatever the conditions in which you are working, there is one resource which is universal and unlimited: the human mind and imagination. This is probably the one single most valuable teaching and learning resource we have. Nothing can replace it. In even the most 'hi-tech' environment, a lack of imagination and humanity will make the most up-to-date and sophisticated resources seem dull; conversely, the most simple resources can be the most exciting and useful.

We have been fortunate to spend quite a lot of our time working not only in 'hi-tech' environments with computers and video, but also in classrooms where there is little more than blackboard and chalk and some out-of-date coursebooks. Some of our most interesting learning and teaching experiences (as Confucius said, a teacher is 'always ready to teach; always ready to learn') have been not in the comfortable well-resourced small classrooms of a private language school, but in classrooms where only the minimum of equipment has been available. Equally, some of our most memorable teaching experiences in 'hi-tech' classrooms have been when we have abandoned the cassette or video or glossy coursebook and got to work with that most precious resource of all, the learners' own experience and imagination.

Teachers often have to use materials which are out of date, or contain subject-matter irrelevant to their particular group of learners. For example, we have had great difficulty explaining the concepts of the fridge-freezer and microwave oven to Tibetans. In the same way, learners who have spent all their lives in northern countries might have difficulty with an exercise from an African textbook which asks if they prefer yam or cassava. So over the last few years we have been trying to design materials which can be used in as wide a range of teaching situations as possible.

The activities we suggest are as flexible as the human imagination is creative; they are 'teacher resource material' which teachers will be able to adjust to suit their particular environment. In thinking about universally applicable, 'lo-tech' materials we have come up with a list of criteria that need to be met. The materials will need to:

- be usable in large classes as well as small.
- be suitable for adult learners as well as secondary learners, and if possible easily adaptable to a primary context.
- be centered on the universals of human experience.

Introduction

- cover the main language skills and have a useful base of grammar and topic vocabulary.
- be traditional enough to be recognizable by all teachers, and thus give them a sense of security, while providing communicative activities for learners.
- be non-threatening in the demands they make on learners.
- be teacher-based 'resource material' rather than books for learners.
- assume that no technical and reprographic resources are available and be based on the human resource rather than the technical.
- be culturally neutral, not context-bound, and thus be flexible, easily adaptable by the teachers to their own culture and teaching context.
- be flexible enough to complement a standard syllabus or coursebook.

Simple Listening Activities

This book contains thirty activities, designed according to the criteria above, for developing the listening skill at elementary level. Each activity has three main stages:

- **Warm-up**—This introduces the learners to the topic and focuses their attention.
- **Listen and respond**—This is the main part of the activity. The learners listen to a text and respond to what they hear in a variety of ways.
- **Follow-up**—This stage gives the learners the opportunity to practise what they have learned using the other language skills.

Warm-up

Before the learners listen to a text, it is very important to prepare them by doing a 'warm-up' activity. This means giving them some idea of what the text is going to be about, either by telling them or asking them to guess.

Before you begin the activity, you may also want to pre-teach difficult new vocabulary. But don't pre-teach all the new vocabulary. Guessing new words is an important listening skill and it is a good idea to give the learners some practice in this. Prepare the text before the lesson and decide which words would be easy for your learners to guess and which would be difficult. Pre-teach only those words which would be difficult or impossible to guess from the context, but which are essential for understanding the text. Leave the others and try to get the learners to guess what they mean—don't do all the work for them! You can explain difficult words or expressions later on in the lesson.

Introduction

Warm-up activities should be very short—they should take not more than about five minutes. All you are aiming to do is to get the learners interested in the topic and familiarize them with some vocabulary.

Listen and respond

Many learners find it difficult to develop the listening skill. Why is this? One reason is that learners may not often hear—or at least need to understand—spoken English outside the classroom. The best way to improve their confidence is to provide them with regular listening practice. It may be that you are worried about your own English, that it is not of 'native speaker' standard. But it is much more important that your learners should have practice in listening than that they should always listen to a so-called 'perfect' model. After all, it is likely that they will often need to understand non-native speakers when they use English in the outside world. If possible, though, it is good for them to have practise in listening to a variety of voices speaking English. In a few activities which include dialogues, for example 5 'Personal information' and 21 'Shopping', we have suggested that you invite a colleague to act out the dialogue with you.

Another reason is that learners try to understand every word and get completely lost, because during the time they have spent worrying about one phrase or word, the speaker has said three or four more sentences. Always ask yourself, 'What is the main message of this text? What are the main points?' Concentrate first of all on helping the learners to understand those main points. Only then, if necessary, should you focus on details of the language.

There are many different techniques which can be used to encourage learners to listen for the main points. For example:

- **Listen and complete**—Learners listen and use the information given to complete a picture, map, diagram, table, or chart.
- **Listen and correct**—Learners listen to a text which contains a number of factual mistakes. They identify and then correct the mistakes.
- **Listen and do**—Learners listen to a series of instructions or actions, and do them as they hear them.
- **Listen and draw**—Learners listen to a description of a person, place, or object and draw it as they listen.
- **Listen and guess**—Learners listen to a description of a person, place, or object and guess what it is.
- **Listen and match**—Learners listen to a description and match it to, for example, pictures, people, objects, or places.

Introduction

- **Listen and reorder**—Learners listen to some information and use it to put some pictures or sentences in the correct order.

There are examples of all these techniques in this book.

Materials

A listening text is provided in most of the activities. This may be in the form of sentences, a descriptive text, or a dialogue. In some cases, it is a good idea to adapt the text to suit your teaching situation and the learners you are working with. For example in 20 'In the market', the lesson will be more interesting for the learners—and they will learn more—if you describe the kinds of food that they see and eat every day. In the case of some texts, especially those where you are describing your own experiences and preferences, for example 22 'Food and drink' it is better if you talk from notes rather than reading out a text. Practise on your own, using just the notes to help you speak, until you feel confident. Even if you do need to follow a text closely, it is important to become familiar with it before the lesson.

In several of the activities, we have provided pictures, plans, or charts for you to copy. These may be drawn on the board, on large pieces of paper ('posters'), or on pieces of card ('flashcards'). In the case of large pictures and plans, posters have obvious advantages over drawings on the board: you can prepare them in advance and they can be stored and used again. Try to find a cheap source of large sheets of paper for posters. In Madagascar, for example, the teachers we worked with found the sheets of paper used for wrapping vegetables in the market were ideal for making posters. A good way to fix posters or flashcards to the board is to pin a length of string along the top of the board like a clothes-line. You can then use clothes-pegs to peg your posters to the string!

Real objects or 'realia' can be used as an alternative to drawings, for example in 12 'Shapes' and 20 'In the market'.

Procedure

During this stage of the activity the learners are first encouraged to listen for the main points in a text, and only after they have done this to listen in detail. The procedure stage has five basic steps:

1 Explain clearly what you want the learners to do and check that they have understood before going on.

2 When you are sure that the learners have understood what to do, read the text or act out the dialogue without stopping. Try to speak as naturally as possible—as if you were telling a story or talking on the telephone—rather than just reading out loud. The first time you present the text, the learners should just listen.

Introduction

3 The second time you present the text, get the learners to do the task while they listen. You may need to read, or act it out, more than once for the learners to complete the task successfully. Again, remember not to stop.

4 Get the learners to check their answers in pairs. Then check the answers yourself with the whole class.

5 Only now is it time for the learners to listen to the text—or parts of it—in detail and for you to help them with the words and expressions that they found hardest to understand. Sometimes you can predict what these will be and have explanations ready, but sometimes you will not know what gave them most difficulty until they tell you. (Alternatively, they might even have found it so easy that you have little explaining to do!) This stage of the lesson involves a lot of interaction between you and the class as you find out what gave them trouble and help them with it. Here are some things you can do at this stage:

- Check the answers and write them on the board as the learners give them to you. Then go over the text again, re-reading the relevant phrases and explaining anything the learners still don't understand.
- Choose some parts of the text to work on in detail, for example a sentence that seemed particularly difficult. Put a series of blanks on the board, one for each word in the sentence:

  _____ _____ _____ _____ _____ .

  (If you want to make this easier, you can write some words in.) Read that part of the text again, asking the learners to fill in as many words as they can. Build up the sentence with the class until all the gaps have been filled.

- When the meaning of a word can be guessed from the context, repeat the phrase or sentence in which it occurs and ask the learners to guess what the word means, or to suggest other words that could replace it.
- Select some useful phrases or expressions from the listening, write them on the board, and ask the learners if they know the meaning. If not, explain it to them.
- Give the learners copies of the listening text or write it on the board. Let them read and listen at the same time. This is a useful technique because it helps them to relate the spoken and the written word. However, don't use it too often, or the learners will put less effort into understanding the text earlier in the activity.

Introduction

Follow-up

If there is time after you have completed the listening activity, you can follow it up with an activity from another skill area, for example speaking or writing. This gives the learners the opportunity to practise what they have learned and helps them establish relationships between the different language skills.

Building a lesson

There are two companion books to this one, *Presenting New Language* and *Simple Speaking Activities*. Each of these also contains thirty activities, and in all three books the topics and the language presented and practised correspond. So, for example, activity 1 in all three books is about 'Greetings and introductions' and activity 30 is about 'Describing actions'. The activities in each book are graded, following a basic structural syllabus. This means that you can design your own lesson or sequence of lessons using material from one, two, or all three books, depending on your learners' needs and the time available.

Activities

1 Greetings and introductions

LANGUAGE	Hello. My name's _____. What's your name? Nice to meet you.
TECHNIQUE	Listen and reorder.
MATERIALS	The dialogue below; the pictures below, on a poster or on the board.
PREPARATION	Prepare the dialogue, if possible with a colleague.
TIME GUIDE	30 minutes.

Warm-up

1 Shake hands with a few learners and greet them in English. Get them to greet you in return.

Listen and reorder

2 Write this mixed-up dialogue on the board and ask the learners to copy it.

What's your name?

Nice to meet you.

My name's Kate.

Nice to meet you too.

Hello. My name's Ben.

3 Tell the class they are going to listen to a dialogue that contains these sentences, but in a different order.

4 If possible, act out the following dialogue with a colleague. Or read it aloud, using different voices for Ben and Kate.

   BEN   Hello. My name's Ben. What's your name?
   KATE   My name's Kate. Nice to meet you.
   BEN   Nice to meet you too.

5 Act out, or read, the dialogue again and ask learners to number the sentences in the order they hear them, like this:

What's your name?	2
Nice to meet you.	4
My name's Kate.	3
Nice to meet you too.	5
Hello. My name's Ben.	1

Greetings and introductions 1

6 Tell the learners to compare their answers with the person sitting next to them. Repeat the dialogue again, so they can check their answers.

7 Put up these pictures. Get the learners to copy them and to write in the dialogue.

8 Ask one or two pairs of learners to read out their sentences in the correct order, one taking Ben's part and the other Kate's (get them to use their own names if they prefer).

Follow-up Tell the learners each to think of someone they would like to be. This could be someone who is well-known locally or nationally, or a person from their country's history. Get them to pretend they are at a party. Tell them to 'introduce' themselves to the learners sitting near them, pretending they are the well-known person they have chosen.

2 The alphabet

LANGUAGE	The letters of the alphabet.
TECHNIQUE	Listen and guess.
MATERIALS	None.
PREPARATION	Choose about ten names of learners in your class.
TIME GUIDE	20 minutes.

Warm-up

1. Spell out your name slowly, letter by letter, writing it on the board as you do so. Ask the learners, 'Whose name is this?' Tell them to try and guess as soon as possible, before you reach the end.

Listen and guess

2. Divide the class into two teams, A and B. Begin to spell out a learner's name. Tell the class to write down the letters as you speak.

3. Tell the class that as soon as anyone thinks they know whose name you are spelling, they should put up their hand. Tell them not to call out the name.

4. The first learner to put up his or her hand may try and guess the name. If he or she is right, his or her team gets a point. If he or she is wrong, the other team gets a point. Continue to spell the name until someone guesses it correctly.

   TEACHER *S – A – R …*
   LEARNER *Sam!*
   (TEAM A)
   TEACHER *No. Team B gets a point. Now listen carefully …*
   – A …
   LEARNER *Sara!*
   (TEAM B)
   TEACHER *Yes, that's right. Team B gets another point.*

5. Spell several names in this way, keeping count of the scores. The team with the most points at the end is the winner.

Follow-up

Get learners to continue the game, spelling out names to each other.

The alphabet 2

Variation

You can also use this activity to revise vocabulary, spelling out words instead of names. At an early stage, when learners do not know much English vocabulary, use words which are the same, or very similar, in English and their own language. Common examples include:

football
hotel
restaurant
taxi
trainers
video

3 Numbers

LANGUAGE	Telephone/phone number.
	Numbers 1 to 9.
TECHNIQUE	Listen and correct.
MATERIALS	A telephone (but this is not essential).
PREPARATION	Prepare about ten telephone numbers.
	Decide which ones you will write down incorrectly.
TIME GUIDE	20 minutes.

Warm-up

1 Write your own, or the school's, telephone number on the board. Say the numbers as you write them. Ask 'What's this?' (Teach 'telephone number' if the learners do not know it. Explain that this is often shortened to 'phone number'.)

2 Ask for volunteers to give you their telephone numbers in English. Write them on the board in figures.

Listen and correct

3 Pretend to be talking on the telephone, for example:

   What's your telephone number? Six – seven – three – five – two – one. Just a minute, let me write that down.

   Write the number on the board in figures.

4 Tell the class that they are going to hear and watch you writing down several more telephone numbers in this way. Tell them that you might make some mistakes. If they think you have made a mistake they should write down the correct number.

5 Repeat the telephone conversation several times with different numbers. Write some correctly, some incorrectly. For example, you might say 'six – seven – three – five – two – *one*', but write:

   6 – 7 – 3 – 5 – 2 – 2

6 Repeat the telephone conversations again. Ask for volunteers to come to the board and correct the numbers you wrote down incorrectly.

Numbers 3

Follow-up

If your class is not too large, make a class telephone directory. Give each learner a list of names of people in the class. Learners should take turns to dictate their telephone number to the rest of the class.

Or, if your learners are unlikely to have telephones at home, prepare a list of up to ten important numbers in your town—for example those of the hospital, the bank, and the station—and write it up on the board. Ask individual learners 'What's the phone number of the _____?' and get them to dictate the number to you.

4 Telling the time

LANGUAGE	What time is it? It's ____ o'clock.
TECHNIQUE	Listen and complete.
MATERIALS	None.
PREPARATION	None.
TIME GUIDE	30 minutes.

Warm-up

1 Draw a clock face on the board, either a round or a digital clock face. Put in a time and ask the class 'What time is it?' Get them to answer 'It's ____ o'clock.' Repeat this with three or four different times.

Listen and complete

2 Draw ten blank clock faces on the board and tell the learners to copy them. Number them 1 to 10.

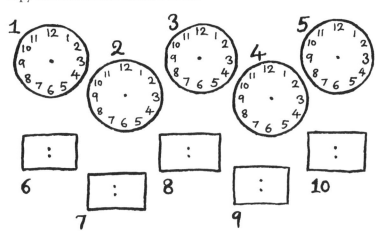

3 Read out the time for each clock, for example:

Clock number one. It's ten o'clock.
Clock number two. It's a quarter to three.

Tell the class just to listen at this stage.

4 Repeat the times. Tell the learners to draw in the hands or write in the numbers on each clock face as you read.

5 Repeat the times once more. Get the learners to compare their answers with the person sitting next to them.

6 Ask individual learners to come up and draw in the hands on the clocks on the board, or write in the numbers.

Telling the time 4

7 When all the clocks on the board are completed, divide the class into two groups for choral practice. Point to different clock faces, getting one group to ask 'What time is it?' and the other group to answer 'It's ___ o'clock', etc.

Follow-up Ask for volunteers to come to the front of the class and draw clock faces showing different times on the board. Get them to ask other learners the time.

5 Personal information

LANGUAGE	What's your name/address? How do you spell that? How old are you? Where are you from? Numbers, alphabet.
TECHNIQUE	Listen and complete.
MATERIALS	The dialogue below.
PREPARATION	Prepare the dialogue below, or a similar one, if possible with a colleague.
TIME GUIDE	40 minutes.

Warm-up

1   Copy this form on the board.

```
NAME .........................................
AGE ...........................................
ADDRESS ..................................
...................................................
PLACE OF BIRTH ....................
```

Ask a learner the following questions:

> What's your name?
> How do you spell that?
> How old are you?
> What's your address?
> Where are you from?

Fill in the form with his or her details.

Listen and complete

2   Rub out the learner's details. Tell the learners to copy the blank form.

3   If possible, act out the following dialogue with a colleague. Alternatively, read it aloud, using different voices for the receptionist and Helen. Tell the learners to listen and note down the kinds of information that they hear about Helen, for example her name and address.

Personal information 5

RECEPTIONIST	Can I help you?
HELEN	Yes, I have an appointment with Dr Bell at ten o'clock.
RECEPTIONIST	Fine. I just need to take your details. What's your name?
HELEN	Browne, Helen Browne. That's Browne with an 'e'—B – R – O – W – N – E.
RECEPTIONIST	And is that Miss or Mrs?
HELEN	Miss.
RECEPTIONIST	Where do you live, Miss Browne? What's your address?
HELEN	29, Alston Road . . .
RECEPTIONIST	How do you spell that, please?
HELEN	A – L – S – T – O – N.
RECEPTIONIST	Thank you. Can you tell me your age please?
HELEN	Sorry?
RECEPTIONIST	How old are you?
HELEN	I'm 17.
RECEPTIONIST	And where are you from?
HELEN	I'm from London.
RECEPTIONIST	Thank you Miss Browne. Please take a seat over there. The doctor will call you in a minute.

4   Act out, or read through, the dialogue again. Ask the learners to compare their answers with the person sitting next to them. They should have Helen's name, address, age, and where she's from.

5   Repeat the dialogue for a third time. This time, tell the learners to fill in the information on their copies of the form.

6   Repeat the dialogue once more so the learners can check their forms.

7   Ask for a volunteer to come and fill in the form on the board. When the form is filled in, repeat the dialogue a final time.

Follow-up

Get learners to make another blank copy of the form. They should then work in pairs. First learner A in each pair should ask learner B for personal information and fill in his or her form, and then learner B should ask learner A.

6 Countries

LANGUAGE	'Countries' vocabulary area (for example, **England, France, Spain**).
TECHNIQUE	Listen and draw.
MATERIALS	Brief description of a world tour; simplified map of the world on a poster, with countries mentioned in the tour marked.
PREPARATION	Prepare a description of a world tour, or use the one below; make a poster of the world map.
TIME GUIDE	40 minutes.

Warm-up   **1**   Put up the map of the world.

Ask the learners which country they would like to visit most.

Listen and draw   **2**   Get the learners to copy the map. Tell them you are going to describe a world tour and ask them to follow your route on their maps.

Countries 6

3 Tell them about your 'travels'. Create a route that includes countries that will be interesting to your learners. Note that they do not need to know the past tense and all the vocabulary in your description. They just need to recognize the names of the countries. Here is an example:

> I left England in June and took a train to France. I stayed there for a few weeks and then went down into Spain. I travelled down into southern Spain and from there I took a boat to South Africa. I stayed there for a while and flew to Australia. I worked in Australia for three months to get money to go to Japan. I visited Japan and China, and from China I took the Trans-Siberian railway home, right across Russia and Germany.

4 Repeat the description and get the learners to mark your route in pencil on their maps.

5 Get the learners to compare their map with that of the person sitting next to them.

6 Repeat the description again, tracing the route with your finger on the poster as you talk.

Follow-up Think of a country and mime or draw something connected with it (for example, eating spaghetti for 'Italy', or a picture of the pyramids for 'Egypt'). Get the learners to guess which country you are thinking of. When you have done two or three mimes or drawings, ask for volunteers to come and mime or draw things connected with other countries for the rest of the class to guess.

7 Nationalities

LANGUAGE	'Nationalities' vocabulary area (for example, **Spanish, French, Italian**).
TECHNIQUE	Listen and complete.
MATERIALS	The description of guests at a party below.
PREPARATION	None.
TIME GUIDE	30 minutes.

Warm-up

1 Write this list of names on the board:

Name	Country	Nationality
Carlos		
Pierre and Annette		
Leonardo		
Hong Mei		
Ahmed		
Sheila		
Sam		

2 Tell the learners that it's a list of guests at an international party. Ask them to guess, from the guests' names, which countries they come from. As the learners guess, fill in the names of the countries in the 'Country' column, for example:

Name	Country	Nationality
Carlos	Spain	
Pierre and Annette	France	
Leonardo	Italy	

Nationalities 7

Listen and complete

3 Tell the learners to copy the list.

4 Tell the learners that they have just arrived at the party. You are going to point out the other guests and say a little about them. Tell the class just to listen for the moment.

> Look over there. The man in the red shirt. That's Carlos, from Barcelona. He's Spanish. Next to Carlos, there's a couple. She's got long hair. That's right. That's Annette and Pierre. They're French … and the man on the left of Pierre is Italian. His name's Leonardo. The girl he's talking to, Hong Mei, is Chinese. Now, over there near the window, can you see the man in the check shirt? That's Ahmed and he's Egyptian. He's talking to a tall man and a blonde woman in a black dress. That's Sam and Sheila. Sheila's Australian and Sam's American.

5 Tell the learners that you are going to describe the other guests again. This time, they should fill in the 'Nationality' column in their copies of the list. Do the first one with them:

Name	_Country_	_Nationality_
Carlos	Spain	Spanish

6 Repeat your description one more time.

7 Fill in the 'Nationality' column on the board and tell the class to check their answers.

Follow-up

Explain that some people arrived late. Ask learners to suggest some more names of guests, with their countries and nationalities, to add to the list.

8 Locating objects

LANGUAGE 'Furniture' (for example, **table**, **chair**, **picture**) and 'everyday objects' (for example, **book**, **pen**, **bag**) vocabulary areas.

Place prepositions (for example, **near**, **in front of**, **on**).

TECHNIQUE Listen and draw.

MATERIALS Description of a living-room; picture of a living-room on the board.

PREPARATION You may want to prepare your own description.

TIME GUIDE 40 minutes.

Warm-up

1 Ask the learners to tell you the English words for furniture and objects that might be found in a living-room. Write their suggestions on the board.

Listen and draw

2 Draw this picture on the board. Tell the learners that it is a living-room.

3 Tell the learners to copy it.

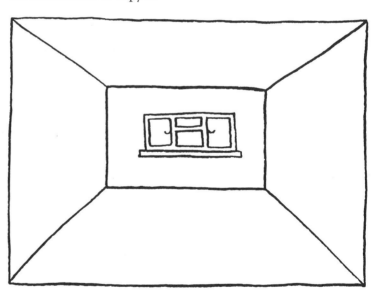

4 Tell the class that you are going to describe the furniture and objects in the room. They must draw the things you describe in the correct places. Do the first one with them.

There's a table near the window.

Pause, and ask the learners to draw the table in their rooms. Get them to use pencils so they can correct any mistakes.

Locating objects 8

5 Draw in the table on the board and check that the learners have drawn their tables in the right place.

6 Tell the learners that you are going to describe the other objects in the room, and that they must draw them in the correct places. Say that you will repeat the description three times. Leave them plenty of time to complete their drawings.

> There's a table near the window, and in front of the table is a chair. There's a picture hanging on the wall by the window. On the table, there's a book and a pen. Under the table there's a bag. There's a box on the floor next to the chair. In the box there's a big, black cat.

7 Ask learners to come to the board and draw in the furniture and objects as you read the text again. The rest of the class should check their drawings.

Follow-up

Rub out all the furniture and objects in the picture on the board leaving just the room and the window. Write the following list on the board:

table	pen
chair	bag
picture	box
book	cat

Ask for volunteers to come to the board and draw these things in different places in the room. Then get the learners to make sentences describing the furniture and objects in their new positions.

9 Feelings

LANGUAGE	'Feelings' vocabulary area (for example, **happy**, **tired**, **angry**).
TECHNIQUE	Listen and match.
MATERIALS	8 flashcards of faces showing different feelings.
PREPARATION	Make the flashcards.
TIME GUIDE	40 minutes.

Warm-up

1 Write two or three English words for feelings on the board, for example:

happy   tired   angry

Ask the learners to think of things that make them have those feelings. Tell them to compare their ideas with a partner. They can use their own language.

Listen and match

2 Put up the flashcards. Give each one a number, for example:

Feelings 9

3 Tell the learners something about each picture, in muddled order, for example:

> Her friend is ill, so she's sad.
> Someone's stolen his watch. He's very angry.
> He's got a special letter today, so he's very happy.
> She's been working in the garden, so she's tired.
> The sun's shining, so he's very hot.
> It's a hot day, so she's very thirsty.
> It's two o'clock. He hasn't had lunch yet, so he's quite hungry.
> She hasn't got a coat, so she's really cold.

4 Tell the learners you are going to repeat the sentences. They should listen carefully and decide which picture each sentence refers to. Tell them not to call out the numbers of the pictures.

5 Repeat the sentences for a third time. This time, tell the learners to write down the numbers of the pictures in the order in which you repeat the sentences.

6 Get the learners to compare their answers in pairs, then check them with the whole class (the order is 4, 3, 1, 2, 5, 7, 8, 6).

Follow-up

Ask a learner to choose one of the pictures, but not to say which one he or she has chosen. The other learners must guess by asking 'Is he happy?', 'Is she sad?', etc.

10 Families

LANGUAGE	'Families' vocabulary area (for example, **mother, father, sister**). Numbers.
TECHNIQUE	Listen and correct.
MATERIALS	The description of a family below; the family tree below on a poster, or on the board.
PREPARATION	Make the poster, if you are using one.
TIME GUIDE	30 minutes.

Warm-up

1 Ask three or four learners questions about their families, for example 'Sam, how many brothers have you got?', 'What's your mother's name, Sara?' Then repeat some of the information making deliberate mistakes. Ask the class to stop you when they hear a mistake, for example:

TEACHER *Sara's mother's name is Anna.*
CLASS   *No it isn't. It's Helen!*

Listen and correct

2 Draw a family tree on the board or put up a poster.

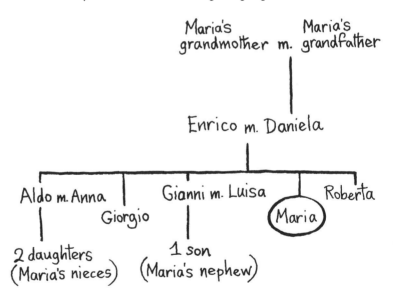

3 Tell the learners to look carefully at the family tree. Ask them one or two questions about it, for example:

How many sisters has Maria got?
What is her father's name?

Families 10

4 Tell the class that you are going to describe Maria's family. Tell them that you might make some mistakes. They should listen very carefully and call out 'Stop!' if they hear any mistakes.

> Maria comes from a large family. She lives with her mother and father and four brothers and sisters. Her father's name is Roberto. He's 45 years old. Her mother's name is Daniela. She's 42 years old. Maria's grandparents—Daniela's mother and father—live with them too. They're quite old now. Her grandmother is 75 and her grandfather is 77. Maria has three brothers, called Aldo, Marco, and Gianni, and one sister called Rosa. Aldo's wife is called Anna, and they have two daughters. Gianni married a girl called Luisa last year and they have a baby daughter.

5 When the learners call out 'Stop!', ask them what the mistake was, and what the correct version should be.

Follow-up Get learners to draw their own family trees (grandparents, parents, any brothers and sisters). Ask for volunteers to talk about their families to the rest of the class. Get them to use 'I've got one/two, _____(s)' and 'My _____'s name is _____.'

11 Colours

LANGUAGE	'Colours' vocabulary area (for example, **orange**, **black**, **blue**).
TECHNIQUE	Listen and match.
MATERIALS	The description of hats and their owners below; the 6 drawings of hats below on a poster, or on the board. (If you are using the board, make sure you have pens or chalks of the colours.)
PREPARATION	Make the poster, if you are using one.
TIME GUIDE	30 minutes.

Warm-up

1 Say the names of some colours and get the learners to tell you the names of objects in the classroom which are that colour.

Listen and match

2 Draw the six hats below on the board, or put up the poster. Number the hats 1 to 6.

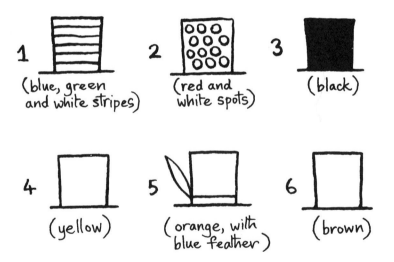

3 Write six names on the board:

Mark

Sara

Sam

Helen

John

Kate

Tell the learners to write down the list of names.

Colours 11

4 Explain to the class that these six people have bought the hats. Unfortunately, the shop assistant has forgotten which hats belong to which person. Tell the class to listen carefully while you describe each hat and say which person it belongs to.

Kate's hat is orange and has a blue feather.

Sam bought a black hat.

Sara wanted a colourful hat and so she bought the one with blue, green, and white stripes.

John chose the one with red and white spots.

Mark bought a lovely yellow hat.

Helen decided to get a brown hat.

5 Tell them to listen to the descriptions again. This time they should write down the numbers of the hats next to the names of the people who bought them.

6 Get the learners to compare their answers with their neighbour.

7 Check the answers with the class (Mark 4; Sara 1; Sam 3; Helen 6; John 2; Kate 5).

Follow-up

Draw two or three more hats on the board. Get the learners to describe them.

12 Shapes

LANGUAGE	'Shapes' vocabulary area (for example, **square**, **round**, **long**).
TECHNIQUE	Listen and match.
MATERIALS	The description of a stolen bag below; the drawings of objects below, on a poster or on the board.
PREPARATION	Make the poster, if you are using one.
TIME GUIDE	30 minutes.

Warm-up

1   Write the following words on the board:

   bag   glasses   handkerchief   diary   pen
   purse   money   stolen

   Make sure the learners understand the meanings of all the words.

2   Ask them to think of a situation in which the words might occur together. Tell them to discuss with a partner, in their own language, what might have happened.

Listen and match

3   Put up the following poster, or do the drawings on the board. Make sure each item in each group of three is labelled A, B, or C.

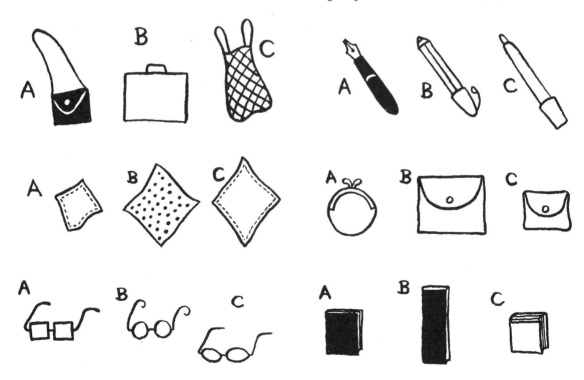

Shapes 12

4 Ask the learners to write down the words: 'bag', 'glasses', 'handkerchief', 'diary', 'pen', and 'purse' in a list.

5 Act the following description, as if you were describing a stolen bag to a police officer on the telephone. Tell the learners to listen to the description and decide which objects in the drawings are being described.

> … Yes, it was this morning at about ten o'clock. I put it down on a chair and the next thing it was gone … yes, yes … my bag. It's made of black leather. It's square. What was in it? Well, my glasses. … They're quite small, with round frames. And a handkerchief. It's large and white. Then there's my diary. It's a long, thin shape … and my pen. Yes, it's a fountain pen. It's short and black and rather old. It was a present from my best friend. And of course my purse was in the bag. It's small, but there was a lot of money in there … about fifty pounds. No, it's not square, it's a round shape. Thank you. I do hope you find it!

6 Tell the learners that you are going to repeat the description. This time they should identify which of the objects in the drawings are being described and write down A, B, or C next to each object in their list.

7 Get the learners to compare their answers with their neighbour.

8 Repeat the description for a third time and check the answers with the class (bag A; pen A; handkerchief C; purse A; glasses B; diary B).

Follow-up

Play 'I spy'. Learners describe an object in the room and the others guess what it is.

Variations

If you have a small class, you could use real bags, pens, handkerchiefs, etc. rather than drawings.

If you can get a colleague to act the part of a police officer, you can turn the description in stage 5 into an interview with the officer asking you questions about the things which have been stolen.

13 Parts of the body

LANGUAGE	'Parts of the body' vocabulary area (for example, **finger, thumb, hand**).
TECHNIQUE	Listen and do.
MATERIALS	The song 'One finger, one thumb, keep moving'; if possible, a guitar or other musical instrument.
PREPARATION	Practise the song.
TIME GUIDE	40 minutes.

Warm-up

1 Draw an outline figure on the board.

Write these words on the board:

finger   thumb   arm   leg   hand   foot   head   nose   eye

Ask for volunteers to come up and label these parts on the figure.

Listen and do

2 Revise or teach the verbs 'move', 'nod', 'twitch', 'wink', and 'jump' by demonstrating the actions. Give a few commands to check that the class have understood, for example:

Move your thumb.
Nod your head.
Twitch your nose.

3 Tell the class you are going to teach them a song. Perform the following verse two or three times. Tell the learners to listen carefully.

Parts of the body 13

4 Repeat, telling the learners to join in, and to move the parts of their bodies mentioned in the song.

5 Add more verses, repeating the notes to fit the words. First the learners should just listen, and then they should join in, performing the actions described in the song. For example:

One finger, one thumb, one arm, one leg, keep moving, (× 3)

One finger, one thumb, one arm, one leg, one hand, one foot, keep moving, (× 3)

One finger, one thumb, one arm, one leg, one hand, one foot, one nod of the head, keep moving, (× 3)

One finger, one thumb, one arm, one leg, one hand, one foot, one nod of the head, one twitch of the nose, keep moving, (× 3)

6 Continue for as many verses as you and your class have invention and energy for!

Follow-up

Tell the learners to work in pairs. Get them to give commands to each other, for example 'Move your hand', 'Wink your eye'.

14 Describing people

LANGUAGE   'Describing people', 'parts of the body', and 'colours' vocabulary areas (for example, **long brown hair**; **small nose**).

TECHNIQUE   Listen and draw.

MATERIALS   The descriptions of people below; coloured pens or chalks.

PREPARATION   None.

TIME GUIDE   40 minutes.

Warm-up

1   Draw a circle on the board.

Ask the learners what it could be. If they have difficulty in guessing 'a face', add a feature, for example an ear or a nose.

2   When they have guessed, ask them to suggest what the face looks like, for example:

TEACHER   *Yes, it's a face. What about the hair? Long? Short?*
LEARNERS   *Long.*
TEACHER   *OK. And what colour?*
LEARNERS   *Brown.* [add long brown hair]
TEACHER   *Now, the nose. Large? Small?*

Complete the face according to the learners' suggestions.

Listen and draw

3   Tell the learners to draw six circles and to label them with the numbers 1 to 6.

4   Tell them you want them to listen and to draw the faces of the six people you describe.

Describing people   14

5 Describe the first person:

> Number one is a man with a beard and short black hair. He's smiling.

Repeat the description and wait for the learners to finish their drawings.

6 Ask for a volunteer to come and copy his or her drawing on the board. Check with the rest of the class that it is the same as the description.

7 Continue with the other descriptions:

> Number two is a man with long fair hair and a beard and glasses. He looks unhappy.
>
> Number three is a boy with very short hair and big ears. He's smiling.
>
> Number four is a woman with long curly hair and glasses. She looks unhappy.
>
> Number five is a happy old lady with white hair, a long nose, and glasses.
>
> Number six is a girl with short curly hair and a big smile.

The learners should draw each person as you describe him or her. Repeat each description and give the learners time to finish their drawings.

8 Ask for volunteers to come and copy their drawings on the board. Check with the rest of the class that they are the same as the descriptions.

Follow-up

Ask individual learners to describe the face of someone in the class. The others should guess who it is.

Variation

Tell the learners to draw six circles, but don't ask them to number them. Read the six descriptions and get the learners to draw the faces. Then tell them to put their pictures up on the wall. Read out the descriptions again and get the learners to match the pictures and the descriptions.

15 Clothes

LANGUAGE	'Clothes' (for example, **T-shirt**, **jeans**, **trainers**) and 'colours' (for example, **blue**, **grey**, **black**) vocabulary areas.
TECHNIQUE	Listen and guess.
MATERIALS	None.
PREPARATION	See stage 2. (If your learners wear uniform, see 'Variation'.)
TIME GUIDE	30 minutes.

Warm-up

1 Tell the learners that you are going to describe someone. They must listen carefully and guess who it is. Tell them to call out the answer as soon as they know. Describe yourself.

Listen and guess

2 At the beginning of the lesson, mentally select five learners and make a note of what they are wearing, both the type and colour of their clothes. (This is so that you do not have to look at them directly while you are describing them later on.)

3 Tell the learners to write the numbers 1 to 5 in their notebooks. Tell them you are going to describe five people in the class. The learners' task is to write the names of those people beside the numbers.

4 Describe each of the learners you have selected, in turn, without looking at them, for example:

> Number one is wearing a blue T-shirt and dark grey jeans. He is also wearing trainers. They are black and white.

Repeat your descriptions, in the same order.

5 Ask the learners to check their answers in pairs.

6 Repeat the descriptions again, pausing after each one and asking the learners to identify their classmates.

Follow-up

Learners take it in turns to describe someone in the class while the others guess who it is.

Clothes 15

Variation

If your learners wear uniform, bring a bag of clothes to class. These should be clothes that the learners can easily put over their uniform, for example hats, jumpers, big T-shirts, and scarves. Choose five learners. Send them outside the room with the clothes while you do the warm-up. They should return dressed up! Stand them in a row at the front and describe one of them. (Try not to look at them too directly while you are speaking.) Ask the rest of the class 'Who is it?' Repeat this procedure with the others.

16 Rooms in a flat

LANGUAGE	'Rooms' vocabulary area (for example, **hall, living-room, kitchen**). **On the right; on the left.**
	Place prepositions (for example, **through, next to, opposite**).
TECHNIQUE	Listen and complete.
MATERIALS	Description of a flat; plan of a flat, on a poster or on the board.
PREPARATION	Make the poster, if you are using one.
TIME GUIDE	30 minutes.

Warm-up

1 Get the learners to think of English words for rooms in a flat or house. Ask them for their suggestions and write the words on the board.

Listen and complete

2 Put up the poster, or draw a plan of a flat on the board:

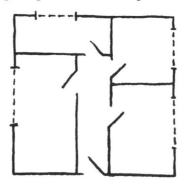

Ask the class for suggestions about which room is which, but don't label the plan.

3 Tell the learners to copy the plan.

4 Tell the learners that this is your flat and that you are trying to sell it. Explain that you are going to describe it to a possible buyer. Their task is to listen to your description and label the rooms. Pretend to be on the telephone talking to the buyer.

> Yes, … it was painted last year. What? Yes, there's a lot of space. You go through the front door into the hall. On the left is the living-room. It's quite big. It's at the front of the building and there's a nice view of the park. Next to the living-room there's the kitchen. Yes … the door's at the end of the hall. What? … No, it's quite small so we always eat in the living-room. There's one bedroom. Yes … that's nice and big. What? Oh, I didn't say … the bedroom's on the right of the hall, opposite the living-room. The bathroom's between the bedroom and the kitchen.

Rooms in a flat 16

5 Repeat your description, then get the learners to work in pairs, comparing how they have labelled their plans.

6 Repeat the description once more, then get a learner to come to the board and write in the names of the rooms as you read the text again.

7 Discuss with the class whether they would like to buy your flat.

Follow-up

Get the learners to draw a plan of their own flat, or—if they live in a house—the ground-floor of their house. They should label all the rooms. Tell them to work in pairs, taking turns to describe their flat or house to the person sitting next to them.

Variation

If your school is in a country area, it might be better to describe a house and not a flat. In any case, adapt the description to suit the kind of home which most of your learners are familiar with.

17 Furniture

LANGUAGE	'Furniture' vocabulary area (for example, **clock**, **sofa**, **table**). Place prepositions (for example, **near**, **round**, **above**).
TECHNIQUE	Listen and complete.
MATERIALS	Instructions for 'removal people'; plan of a living-room on the board.
PREPARATION	You may want to prepare your own instructions and plan.
TIME GUIDE	40 minutes.

Warm-up

1 Tell the learners to stand up. Ask them to imagine that they are moving house. Tell them to pick up different pieces of furniture, some heavy and some light, for example:

> Here's a little clock. Can you pick it up? Be careful, it's not very heavy but it's very valuable. Here's a sofa. Can you lift it? It's heavy. Ask someone to help you … etc.

Listen and complete

2 Clear a space in the classroom. Ask the learners to imagine that it is a living-room in a new house. Show them where the door and window are. Tell them that the room is empty at the moment. Some furniture has been delivered and needs to be arranged in the room.

3 Ask for two volunteers to act as 'removal people'. Their task is to mime the actions as you tell them what to do with the furniture, for example:

> Carry the table through the door—careful! Can you put it near the window. Thanks! Now the chairs—those four chairs. [*point to imaginary chairs*] OK. Can you put them round the table? OK. Now the sofa. Be careful. That sofa's very heavy! Put the sofa by that wall there please. Now the armchair. Next to the sofa. OK. What's next? Ah, the picture. Put that on the wall above the sofa. Fine. And the television. That needs to go opposite the sofa and the armchair. Finally—the cupboard. That goes in the corner, behind the door. Oh yes, this vase. Put that on the cupboard.

Tell the rest of the class to listen and watch carefully.

4 When all the imaginary furniture is in place, draw an outline plan of the room on the board and tell the learners to copy it.

Furniture 17

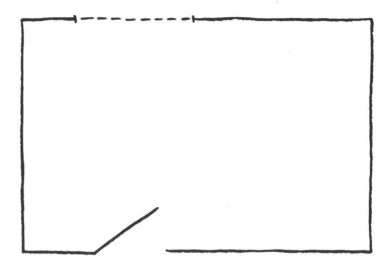

5 Ask the learners to try and remember the position of all the pieces of furniture in the room. Tell them to draw the furniture in the correct places on their plans and label it, like this:

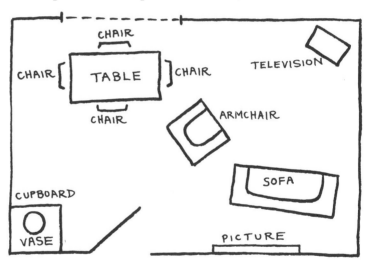

6 Ask for volunteers to come and draw the pieces of furniture in the outline room on the board. The rest of the class should check their plans.

Follow-up

Ask the learners to suggest changes in the arrangement of the furniture. Learners who have ideas for changes should come to the board, alter the plan, and describe their changes in English.

18 In town

LANGUAGE	'Town' vocabulary area (for example, **street, cinema, cafe**). Place prepositions (for example, **opposite, next to, beside**). **On the right; on the left.**
TECHNIQUE	Listen and complete.
MATERIALS	Description of a town centre; simple plan of a town centre, on a poster or on the board.
PREPARATION	You may want to prepare your own instructions and plan. Make the poster, if you are using one.
TIME GUIDE	40 minutes.

Warm-up 1 Put up a plan of a town centre on the board, for example:

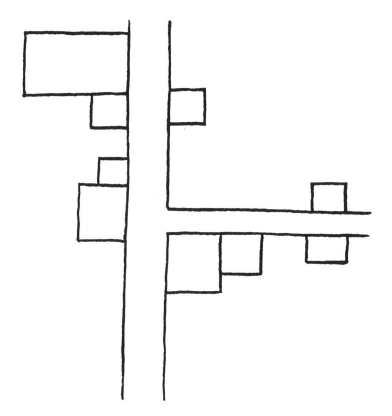

Ask the learners to tell you English words for shops and other places they might find in a town centre. Write these up in a list on the board. Explain any words that learners don't understand.

18 In town

Listen and complete

2 Tell the learners to copy the plan. Then describe the town centre to them. The first time you give the description, tell them just to listen.

> You've never been to Newton? Well, the centre's quite small. Main Street is the biggest street. It runs north–south. [*pause*] Then there's Old Street which is much smaller. As you go north up Main Street, Old Street is on the right. [*pause*] Opposite the junction of Main Street and Old Street, there's a big cinema. [*pause*] Next to the cinema, there's a little cafe. It sells very good ice-cream. [*pause*] Continue north up Main Street, and there's a hotel with a large car-park beside it. [*pause*] Then opposite the hotel there's a post office. [*pause*] Shops? Most of them are in Old Street. If you go along Old Street from Main Street, the first shop on the right is a newsagent. [*pause*] Then next to the newsagent there's a butcher. [*pause*] Opposite the butcher there's a little baker's shop. [*pause*] Oh, I forgot the library. That's on the south side of Old Street, on the corner with Main Street.

3 Read the description again, leaving pauses for the learners to label the places. Tell them to label as many places as they can, but not to worry if they can't label all of them.

4 Read the description for a third time. This time the learners should try and label all the places.

5 Ask for a volunteer to come to the board and label the plan as you read the description slowly. The rest of the class should check their plans.

Follow-up

Get the class to look again at the list of places you wrote on the board in the warm-up. Are there any places the learners suggested that were not included in your description of the plan—for example a bank, a supermarket, a park? Get learners to come to the board and add these to the plan. Ask them to describe where they are, for example 'The bank is between the cafe and the hotel.'

19 Directions

LANGUAGE	Go straight on. Turn right. Turn left. Take the second on the right. Take the third on the left.
TECHNIQUE	Listen and match.
MATERIALS	The directions below; the plan of a town centre below, on a poster or on the board.
PREPARATION	Prepare the poster, if you are using one.
TIME GUIDE	40 minutes.

Warm-up

1 Draw these signs on the board:

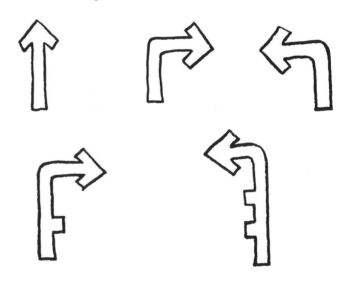

Ask for a volunteer to come to the board. Give these directions in random order:

Go straight on.
Turn right.
Turn left.
Take the second on the right.
Take the third on the left.

Tell the volunteer to point to the appropriate sign when you give a direction.

Directions 19

Listen and match

2   Draw this plan on the board, or put up the poster. Point out the arrow labelled 'YOU ARE HERE'.

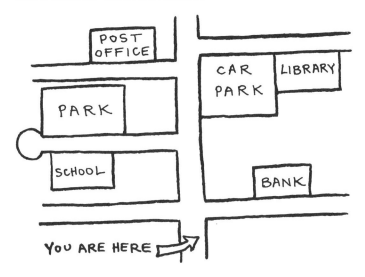

3   Ask the learners to write the numbers 1 to 5 in their notebooks.

4   Explain to the class that you are going to give directions from the arrow labelled YOU ARE HERE to five places on the map. Give directions to the first place:

  Number one. Go straight on. Take the third on the left. Then it's on your right.

  Tell the learners to write down the name of the place. Check that they have got 'post office'.

5   Do the same for the other four places.

  Number two. Go straight on. Take the second on the right. Go past the car park, then it's on your right.

  Number three. Take the first on the right, then it's on the left.

  Number four. Take the second on the left. It's near the end of the road on the right.

  Number five. Take the second on the left. It's opposite the park.

6   Repeat all the directions, then tell the learners to check their answers in pairs (2 library; 3 bank; 4 park; 5 school).

7   Ask individual learners to come to the front and trace each route on the map with a finger as you give each direction.

Follow-up Ask learners to give directions to other places on the map.

45

20 In the market

LANGUAGE	'Food' vocabulary area (for example, **carrots**, **tomatoes**, **honey**).
	Some, any.
TECHNIQUE	Listen and guess.
MATERIALS	6 food items that are available in your local market. Include countable and uncountable foods.
PREPARATION	Collect the food items. Prepare short, simple descriptions of them like the ones below.
TIME GUIDE	30 minutes.

Warm-up

1 Ask the learners to think of three kinds of food they can buy in the local market and write them down. Tell them to write the English words if they know them. Collect their suggestions and write them in a list on the board. If they don't know the English word, translate for them.

Listen and guess

2 Place the six items you have brought to class on your desk where everyone can see them. Explain that this is your 'market'.

3 Check the list on the board with the class. Are there any items in your market which are not on the list? If so, add them.

4 Describe an item on the list without mentioning its name. Say whether it is in the market or not. For example:

These are long and orange. There aren't any in the market today.

Ask the learners to guess which item you are talking about. When they have guessed (carrots), tell them to write the numbers 1 to 8.

5 Describe eight more items on the list without mentioning their names. Include four items in your market and four from the list. For example:

Number one. These are round and red. There are some in the market today. (tomatoes)

Number two. This is yellow and sticky. It is very sweet and you put it on bread. There's some in the market today. (honey)

Number three. This is white and you can drink it. It comes from cows. There isn't any in the market today. (milk)

Number four. These are long and yellow. There aren't any in the market today. (bananas)

Number five. These are round and orange. They are sweet. There are some in the market today. (oranges)

In the market 20

> Number six. These are round and brown. They grow in the earth. There aren't any in the market today. (potatoes)
>
> Number seven. This is yellow. It comes from cows and you put it on bread. There's some in the market today. (butter)
>
> Number eight. This comes from the sea. There isn't any in the market today. (fish)

The learners should guess what the items are and write the answers beside the numbers.

6 Repeat the descriptions and ask the learners to compare their answers in pairs.

7 Ask for a volunteer to come to the front of the class. Tell him or her to point to each food item in the list as you describe it. If the item is in your market, hold it up. Check the answers with the class.

Follow-up

Get the learners to make up descriptions for the remaining items in the list. Help them if necessary.

21 Shopping

LANGUAGE	Typical language used in shopping.
	'Containers' and 'food and drink' vocabulary areas (for example, **a kilo of tomatoes, a jar of jam, a bag of flour**).
TECHNIQUE	Listen and match.
MATERIALS	Shopping list; dialogue.
PREPARATION	You may want to adapt the shopping list and dialogue. If possible, prepare to act the dialogue with a colleague.
TIME GUIDE	40 minutes.

Warm-up

1 Introduce the idea of a 'shopping list'. Ask the learners what things they might put on their shopping list for one of the following: a popular national dish in your country; a meal to celebrate an important festival; a family of five young children.

2 Collect their suggestions and write them on the board. If they don't know the English word, translate for them.

Listen and match

3 Write a shopping list on the board, for example:

tomatoes

plum jam

flour

oranges

sugar

Tell the learners to copy it.

4 Write up a list of quantities and containers beside the shopping list, like this:

tomatoes	*1 kg*
plum jam	*4*
flour	*1 jar*
oranges	*1 bag*
sugar	*2 kgs*

48

Shopping 21

5 The learners should copy this as well. Ask them to suggest which measurement or container goes with which food. There may be more than one possibility.

6 Read this dialogue or, if possible, act it with a colleague. Tell the learners to listen carefully and find out which measurements and containers go with which foods.

ASSISTANT Good morning. Can I help you?
CUSTOMER Good morning. Have you got any oranges today?
ASSISTANT Yes, how many would you like?
CUSTOMER Four please.
ASSISTANT Here you are. Anything else?
CUSTOMER Yes, tomatoes. A kilo of tomatoes please.
ASSISTANT These here or those ones over there?
CUSTOMER These'll do thanks.
ASSISTANT One kilo of tomatoes. Anything else?
CUSTOMER Yes, I need some jam.
ASSISTANT Strawberry? Raspberry?
CUSTOMER Er … have you got any plum jam?
ASSISTANT Yes, here you are. One jar was it?
CUSTOMER Yes, thanks. Erm … what else? … some flour. I'd better have two kilos, I think. And I need sugar too. One of those small bags of sugar.
ASSISTANT Will that be all?
CUSTOMER Yes, thank you. How much is that?
ASSISTANT That'll be four pounds exactly please.

7 Read or act the dialogue again. This time, tell the learners to match the foods with the measurements and containers by drawing lines between them in their lists.

8 Ask a pair who are confident with their answers to come to the board and draw the lines between the two lists. Read or act the dialogue once more.

Follow-up

Ask each learner to think of a dish they know how to cook. Get them to write down a list of the ingredients (help them with the English words if necessary). Tell them to work in pairs. They should read their lists to each other without saying the name of the dish. Can their partner guess what they are 'cooking'?

22 Food and drink

LANGUAGE	'Food and drink' vocabulary area (for example, **fish, pasta, oranges**). I like _____. I don't like _____. **Very much; quite; not very much; not at all.**
TECHNIQUE	Listen and complete.
MATERIALS	A short talk about your likes and dislikes in food; the chart below on the board.
PREPARATION	Prepare notes for a short talk like the one below. Mention 10 to 15 different kinds of food. It is more interesting for the learners if what you say is true!
TIME GUIDE	40 minutes.

Warm-up

1 Find out the most popular food in the class. Ask each learner to name their favourite food. Write these on the board and mark the total number of learners who like that food underneath, for example:

ice-cream	hamburgers	fish
/ / / / /	/ / / / / / / /	/ /

Listen and complete

2 Draw this chart on the board and tell the learners to copy it:

very much	quite	not very much	not at all

3 Tell the class that you are going to talk about the kinds of food you like and dislike. Tell them to listen and fill in the chart with the names of the foods in the correct columns. It is best if you talk informally from notes rather than preparing a text. Here is an example:

> Well, my favourite dish is fish. I like fish very much—all kinds of fish, especially shellfish like shrimps or crab. I don't like meat very much so I don't eat it often, though I quite like chicken so I do eat that sometimes. I quite like pasta and vegetables, but there's one vegetable I don't like at all—that's cauliflower. I eat a lot of fruit—for breakfast, lunch, and dinner. I like most kinds of fruit very much. My favourites are mangoes and papaya, but I really don't like oranges at all.

Food and drink 22

4 Repeat the talk. Don't worry about repeating it word for word, but make sure your likes and dislikes are the same! Tell the learners to check their answers with their neighbour.

very much	quite	not very much	not at all
fish	chicken	meat	cauliflower
shrimps	pasta		oranges
crab	vegetables		
fruit			
mangoes			
papaya			

5 Ask for volunteers to come to the board and fill in the names of the foods in the correct columns.

Follow-up

Tell the learners to work in pairs. Write this sentence frame on the board:

We like _____ very much, and we quite like _____, but we don't like _____ at all.

Tell them to find out what kinds of food they both like very much, what they both quite like, and what they both don't like at all. They should then fill the gaps to make a sentence that is true for both of them.

Variation

If you can get a colleague to come in and be interviewed about food, this would make a good additional or alternative listening activity to the one above. Explain to your colleague before the lesson that you would like him or her to use the expressions 'very much', 'quite', 'not very much', and 'not at all' when describing preferences. Ask questions like the following:

What's your favourite food?
What's your least favourite food?
Do you eat much meat?

23 Leisure activities

LANGUAGE	'Leisure activities' vocabulary area (for example, **table tennis, swimming, sewing**).
	I love/like/don't like/hate _____.
TECHNIQUE	Listen and complete.
MATERIALS	A short talk about the things you do in your spare time; a chart like the one below on the board.
PREPARATION	Prepare notes for a short talk, like the one below, about the kinds of leisure activity you like and dislike. Mention 5 to 10 activities. It is more interesting for the learners if what you say is true!
TIME GUIDE	40 minutes.

Warm-up   **1**   Write a list of about ten leisure activities on the board. Choose ones that your learners take part in themselves. Tell the class that you want them to divide the activities into two groups. They can do this in any way they like. Give them one or two suggestions, for example:

> activities they like – activities they dislike
> sports – other activities

Encourage them to think of their own ideas. Get them to work in pairs or small groups. After about five minutes, ask them for their suggestions.

Listen and complete   **2**   Explain that you are going to talk about the things you do in your spare time. Tell the learners to listen and see how many of their guesses were right! It is best if you talk informally from notes rather than preparing a text. Here is an example:

> I like a game of table tennis occasionally and I'm quite good at it—though I'm terrible at tennis! I don't like tennis at all. In the summer I love swimming, especially in the sea. I love playing badminton but I'm not very good at it, although I practise a lot. Apart from sport, my other main hobby is sewing—I really enjoy a quiet evening at my sewing machine. My sister's very interested in chess and she's always trying to get me to play, but I hate it.

Leisure activities 23

3 Draw this chart on the board and tell the learners to copy it:

	love	like	don't like	hate
badminton				
chess				
sewing				
swimming				
table tennis				
tennis				

4 Tell the class that you are going to talk about the things you do in your spare time again. This time they should tick the appropriate boxes in their charts. Stop and check after the first activity that you mention to see that they understand.

5 Ask for volunteers to come to the board and tick the appropriate boxes.

Follow-up

Get learners to think of one activity they love, one they like, one they don't like, and one they hate. Take a vote to find out which are the most and which are the least popular activities in the class.

24 Daily routines

LANGUAGE	'Everyday actions' vocabulary area (for example, **get up, have supper, go to sleep**).
TECHNIQUE	Listen and correct.
MATERIALS	A story about a daily routine containing mistakes, like the one below; the correct version.
PREPARATION	Write a story, or use the one below. If you write your own story, remember to prepare a correct version.
TIME GUIDE	30 minutes.

Warm-up

1 Put the title 'Peter's day' on the board. Ask the learners to tell you what they think he or she does every day. Prompt them with questions, for example 'What does Peter do first every day?', etc.

Listen and correct

2 Read a short story of a mixed-up day to the learners, for example:

Every day I get up at midday. First I go to the cinema and then I have supper. Then I go to sleep. After that I fly to school. I have lunch at seven o'clock and I go home at one o'clock. In the morning, I cook breakfast and then brush my teeth. I wake up at ten thirty.

3 Tell them that you are going to read the story again. This time, tell them to put up their hand every time they hear a mistake and to correct it with more suitable words.

4 Write the story on the board with gaps for the mistakes, for example:

Every day I get up at _____. First I _____ and then I _____. Then I _____. After that I _____ to school. I have lunch at _____ o'clock and I go home at _____ o'clock. In the _____, I cook _____ and then _____. I _____ at ten thirty.

5 Ask for volunteers to come up and write in suitable words. The 'correct' version might look like this:

Every day I get up at six thirty. First I wash and then I have breakfast. Then I brush my teeth. After that I walk to school. I have lunch at one o'clock and I go home at five o'clock. In the evening, I cook supper and then watch TV. I go to bed at ten thirty.

Daily routines

Follow-up Prepare a simple story of the daily routine of someone the learners all know, or who has a familiar job such as a postman or a doctor. It should contain no more than five or six sentences. Write the sentences in random order on the board and get the learners to put them in the right order.

25 Jobs

LANGUAGE   'Jobs' vocabulary area (for example, **postman**, **dentist**, **waiter**).
TECHNIQUE   Listen and guess.
MATERIALS   The short descriptions of jobs below.
PREPARATION You might want to adapt, or add to, the descriptions.
TIME GUIDE 30 minutes.

Warm-up

1 Write up the following words on the board:

   delivers   uniform   cap

   apron   scissors   needle

   drives   makes   uses   coat

   Ask the learners to divide them into these three groups:

   things we do
   things we use
   things we wear

2 Explain any unfamiliar words. Then ask the class what they think the listening text will be about.

Listen and guess

3 Tell the learners to write the numbers 1 to 6. Tell them you are going to describe six jobs without mentioning the names of the jobs. They must guess the jobs you are describing.

4 Read the six descriptions. Tell the learners just to listen and not to write anything for the moment.

   Number one. He wears a uniform and drives a van or rides a bicycle. He gets up very early in the morning to deliver letters to people's houses.

   Number two. You go and see this person when you have toothache. He or she wears a white coat and uses a drill.

   Number three. This person brings you food and drink when you are in a restaurant.

   Number four. She wears a uniform and works in a hospital. She cares for people when they are ill.

   Number five. He makes clothes for men. He has a shop where he sells the clothes.

   Number six. He wears a white coat and sometimes a white hat. He makes bread and cakes and sells them in a shop.

Jobs 25

5 Read the descriptions again. This time, the learners should write down the names of the jobs.

6 Repeat the descriptions once more. Tell the learners to check their answers in pairs.

7 Ask for volunteers to come and write the answers on the board (1 postman; 2 dentist; 3 waiter/waitress; 4 nurse; 5 tailor; 6 baker).

Follow-up

Get the learners to make their own descriptions of jobs. Put these substitution tables on the board to help them:

He	works	indoors.
She		outdoors.

He	wears	smart clothes.
She		a uniform.
		a white coat.

He	mends	_____ .
She	makes	
	sells	
	grows	
	looks after	

They should think of a job and choose words from the framework to describe it. Ask individual learners to read out their descriptions and get other learners to guess the job.

26 Housework

LANGUAGE	'Housework' vocabulary area (for example, **wash the dishes**, **sweep the floor**, **polish the furniture**).
TECHNIQUE	Listen and complete.
MATERIALS	The 'crazy housework' story below; the timetable below on the board.
PREPARATION	None.
TIME GUIDE	40 minutes.

Warm-up

1 Write up a list of four or five 'housework' verbs, for example:

wash

sweep

polish

clean

Ask the learners for a noun to go with each verb. Examples are 'dishes', 'floor', 'furniture', and 'windows'.

Listen and complete

2 Tell the class that you are going to read them a story called 'Crazy housework'. Ask them to suggest what it might be about.

3 Read the story.

> My uncle lives on his own and his house is a real mess. Last Saturday I went to see him and I spent the whole day doing his housework for him. First of all I washed his shirts. He tried to stop me. 'I always polish my clothes on Thursdays!' he said. 'I can manage by myself' he said, 'I'm very organized. I cook the beds on Mondays and I iron the floor on Tuesdays. I dry the shopping on Wednesdays and on Fridays I usually make the windows. And on Saturdays I feed the furniture.' 'What do you do on Sundays?' I asked him. He stared at me. 'Are you crazy?' he said. 'I never do any housework on Sundays. I listen to a walk in the park, or I sometimes watch a book at home.'

Were any of the learners' suggestions right?

58

Housework **26**

4 Write up a timetable for the week on the board.

Mon	Tue	Wed	Thur	Fri	Sat	Sun

Tell the learners to copy it.

5 Tell the learners that you are going to repeat the story. As they listen again they should try to write in the uncle's crazy housework timetable. When they have finished it should look like this:

Mon	Tue	Wed	Thur	Fri	Sat	Sun
cook beds	iron floor	dry shopping	polish clothes	make windows	feed furniture	listen to walk watch book

6 Tell the learners to imagine that they are his nephews or nieces. They should correct his timetable and make a more sensible one for him.

7 Ask for volunteers to come to the board to make the corrections.

Follow-up Get the learners to write their own (sensible) timetables.

27 Abilities

LANGUAGE	Verbs for common actions. **Can, can't.**
TECHNIQUE	Listen and guess.
MATERIALS	The riddles below.
PREPARATION	You might like to think of more riddles and add them to the ones below.
TIME GUIDE	30 minutes.

Warm-up

1 Introduce the topic of riddles. Ask the learners the Sphinx's riddle: 'What moves on four legs in the morning, two legs in the day, and three legs in the evening?' (Answer: a man going from being a baby crawling to a man walking, and then becoming an old man who walks with a stick.) Ask the class if they know any riddles in their own language.

Listen and guess

2 Tell the learners to write the numbers 1 to 5. Say you are going to tell them five riddles. They must try and think of the person, animal, or thing you are describing.

> Number one. I can't talk or walk. I can't eat but I can drink. I can smile and cry. Who am I?
>
> Number two. I've got four legs but I can't walk. What am I?
>
> Number three. I can go out for a walk, but I can't leave my house. I can only walk very slowly. What am I?
>
> Number four. I've got feathers but I can't fly. I can keep you warm at night, though. What am I?
>
> Number five. I've got hands, but I can't lift anything. I've got a face but I can't see, hear, or speak. I can tell you the time though. What am I?

3 Read the riddles a couple of times, leaving time for the learners to write down the answers.

4 Read the riddles for a third time, pausing after each one to allow the whole class to call out the answer (1 a baby; 2 a table; 3 a tortoise, or a snail; 4 a duvet; 5 a clock, or a watch).

Abilities 27

Follow-up

Get learners to work in pairs, making up their own riddles using 'can' and 'can't'. Suggest some subjects they could make riddles about and help them with English vocabulary, for example:

a needle	it has an 'eye'
a saw	it has 'teeth'
a nail	it has a 'head'
a chair	it has 'legs', a 'back', and sometimes 'arms'

28 Rules: 'must' and 'mustn't'

LANGUAGE	'Jobs' vocabulary area (for example, **teacher, doctor, policeman**). **Must, mustn't**.
TECHNIQUE	Listen and match.
MATERIALS	The extracts from conversations below.
PREPARATION	None.
TIME GUIDE	30 minutes.

Warm-up

1 Introduce the topic of school rules. Ask the learners for examples of things they must and mustn't do at school. Help them translate their ideas into English if necessary.

Listen and match

2 Write the following words on the board in two lists, A and B, like this:

A	B
teacher	driver
doctor	passenger
policeman	patient
librarian	pupil
ticket collector	student

3 Explain any unfamiliar words. Choose some examples from list B, for example 'patient' and 'driver'. Ask what kinds of things these people must and mustn't do.

4 Get the learners to copy the two lists, side by side.

5 Tell them they are going to hear five short extracts from conversations. In each extract, someone from list A is talking to someone from list B. They must decide who is talking, and who they are talking to.

6 Read the extracts. Try and 'act' them as much as possible, using appropriate intonation and gestures.

> Number one. You're late again! You must try to get to school on time.

> Number two. You mustn't park in this street. Look at the notice up there! I'm afraid you must pay a fine of twenty pounds, and you must pay it before next Friday.

Rules: 'must' and 'mustn't' 28

Number three. You must stop smoking, and you mustn't eat so many sweets. … And you really must try to take more exercise.

Number four. Shhh! You must be quiet. … And you mustn't bring any food or drink in here.

Number five. No sir. You must have a ticket before starting your journey. No, I'm sorry. You must get off the train at the next station.

7 Read the extracts again. This time, tell the learners to draw a line between who is talking and who they are talking to.

8 Read the extracts for a third time so the learners can check their answers.

9 Ask for a volunteer to come to the board and draw the lines between the two lists (1 teacher – pupil; 2 policeman – driver; 3 doctor – patient; 4 librarian – student; 5 ticket collector – passenger).

Follow-up

Tell the learners to work in pairs. Ask each pair to choose one of the five extracts above. Get them to make up three more 'rules' for that situation in that extract (for example, teacher – pupil) using 'must' and/or 'mustn't'. Each pair should read out their rule and the rest of the class should guess the situation.

29 Describing actions 1

LANGUAGE   Present continuous.
TECHNIQUE Listen and guess.
MATERIALS The short descriptions of places below.
PREPARATION You may want to adapt, or add to, the descriptions below.
TIME GUIDE 30 minutes.

Warm-up

1 Ask the learners to guess what place it is you are describing. Describe the classroom scene as it is now, for example:

A man/woman is standing in a large room. There are a lot of people in front of him/her. They are all sitting down. Someone is _____ing. Someone else is _____ing, etc. [*Describe what a few learners are actually doing.*]

Continue with your description until the learners guess. Don't make it too easy for them!

Listen and guess

2 Tell the learners that you are going to describe five scenes to them. Tell them to listen and, for each scene, decide either 'What is happening?' or 'Where is it?'

Number one. My garden is full of people. My little sister is crying. My father is bringing a ladder and everyone is looking up into a tree. What is happening?

Number two. The room is full of people. There is loud music playing. Some people are eating and some people are drinking. A lot of people are dancing. What is happening?

Number three. My friend is lying in bed in a long room. A lot of other people are lying in bed too. Some of them are listening to the radio. Some of them are talking to friends. One is talking to a man in a white coat. And a lot of people are sleeping. Where is my friend?

Number four. I'm in a big building. A lot of people are sitting behind a long counter. Other people are queuing at the counter and writing on pieces of paper. Some of them are collecting a lot of money! Where am I?

Number five. I'm in a big building. A lot of people are sitting behind a long counter. Other people are queuing at the counter with letters and parcels. They are buying small, brightly coloured pieces of paper and sticking them on the letters and parcels. Where am I?

Describing actions 1   29

3 Ask the learners to write the numbers 1 to 5. Read the descriptions of the scenes again, this time leaving pauses between each description so the learners can write down the answers.

4 Read the descriptions a once more. This time, get the learners to check their answers with their neighbour.

5 Check the answers with the class (1 my little brother is stuck up a tree; 2 at a party; 3 in a hospital; 4 in a bank; 5 in a post office).

Follow-up

Write the following sentence frames on the board:

I'm _____ing.

Some people are _____ing.

Other people are _____ing.

One man/woman is _____ing.

Tell the learners to work in pairs. Ask them to imagine that they are at a place in town. Tell them write a description of this place by copying the sentence frames and filling the blanks. Then ask each pair to read out their description. The rest of the class should guess the place they are describing.

30 Describing actions 2

LANGUAGE	'Town' vocabulary area (for example, **shop**, **cafe**, **bank**).
	Present continuous.
TECHNIQUE	Listen and do.
MATERIALS	The description of a street scene below.
PREPARATION	You may want to adapt the description below.
TIME GUIDE	40 minutes.

Warm-up

1 Tell the learners to think of the main street in your town or village. Ask them what kinds of building they can find there. Write the English words on the board.

Procedure

2 Create a 'street' at the front of the class by arranging chairs and desks to stand for a shop, a cafe, a bank, and a bus stop. Describe it to the learners, for example:

> This is the main street. This is the butcher's shop here. And here, next to the butcher's, there's a cafe. There are tables and chairs outside the cafe. On the other side of the cafe, there's a bank. And here's the bus stop, by the bank.

3 Describe the following scene. Ask the learners to imagine the events taking place on the 'street' in front of them.

> I'm looking out of my window. There's a busy street outside. Opposite me a man and two boys are standing at the bus stop. The man is reading a newspaper. The two boys are eating sweets out of a bag. A woman is coming out of the butcher's shop. She's carrying a very heavy basket. A man is sitting at the cafe next to the butcher's, drinking coffee and writing in a notebook. There are two girls sitting at the table next to him. One is eating spaghetti and the other is eating ice-cream. A young woman is walking down the street with a small dog on a lead. I can see two men coming out of the bank. They are carrying a big, heavy bag. I wonder what is inside?

4 Ask ten learners to come to the front of the class. Position them in your street, three at the bus stop, one coming out of the butcher's shop, three sitting outside the cafe, and so on. Tell them that when you read the description again, you want them to form a tableau (i.e. a three-dimensional picture) of the scene.

5 Describe the scene again. The ten learners should form the tableau as you read.

Describing actions 2 — 30

6 Tell the ten learners to return to their places. See how many details the class can remember and repeat to you in English.

Follow-up

Get the learners to write seven sentences to form a description of the scene. Can they remember what all the people were doing? If they need help, you can remind them by writing these prompts on the board:

A man . . .

Two boys . . .

A woman . . .

A man . . .

Two girls . . .

A young woman . . .

Two men . . .